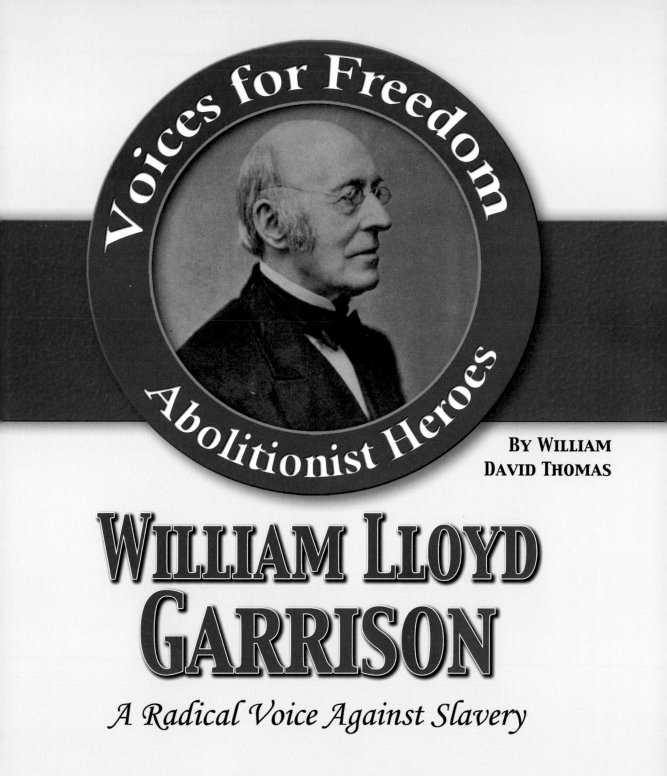

Voices for Freedom

Abolitionist Heroes

By William
David Thomas

WILLIAM LLOYD GARRISON

A Radical Voice Against Slavery

CRABTREE
Publishing Company
www.crabtreebooks.com

Author: William David Thomas
Publishing plan research and development:
 Sean Charlebois, Reagan Miller
 Crabtree Publishing Company
Editors: Mark Sachner, Lynn Peppas
Proofreader: Ellen Rodger
Editorial director: Kathy Middleton
Photo research: Ruth Owen
Designer: Westgrapix/Tammy West
Production coordinator: Margaret Amy Salter
Production: Kim Richardson
Curriculum adviser: Suzy Gazlay, M.A.
Editorial consultant: James Marten, Ph.D.; Chair, Department
 of History, Marquette University, Milwaukee, Wisconsin

Front cover (inset), back cover, and title page: Photograph of
William Lloyd Garrison in his later years.
Front cover (bottom): A series of anti-slavery trading cards from
the 1800s, by American artist Henry Louis Stephens. Pictures like
this were used by abolitionists to convince people that slavery
should be stopped.

Written, developed, and produced by Water Buffalo Books

Publisher's note:

Photographs and reproductions
Alamy: page 6 (right); page 12. Getty Images: Rischgitz: page 6
 (left); page 16; Al Fenn: page 17 (bottom); Rischgitz: page 25
 (top); page 28 (bottom); page 29 (top); page 31 (top); Herbert
 Orth: page 34 (bottom); Karen Bleier: page 48;
 page 58 (bottom).
The Granger Collection: page 38. The Liberator Files: page 13;
 page 19 (bottom); page 21; page 24; page 29 (center right); page
 29 (center left); page 32; page 34 (top); page 35; page 36; page
 42; page 56 (top).
Courtesy of the Library of Congress: Image 3a12743; page 3; page
 4 (top left); Image 3a20849: page 7; Image 3b23576: page 10;
 Image 3a12743: page 12 (top left); Image 3b27512: page 15;
 Image 3a12743: page 19 (top left); Image 3g03254: page 20 (left);
 Image 3g02524: page 22; Image 3a04601: page 23 (top); Image
 3b36893: page 23 (bottom); Image 3a44497: page 26: Image
 3a12743: page 28 (top left); Image 3a12743: page 35 (top left);
 Image 3a12898: page 37 (top); Image 1184: page 37 (bottom);
 Image 3a18122: page 39; Image 3b39466: page 40; Image
 3a10453: page 41 (top); Image 3a12743: page 43 (top left); Image
 3b37099: page 45; Image 3c37591: page 46; Image 3a36987: page
 47; Image 3a12743: page 50 (top left); Image 3g05341: page 53;
 Image 3c19343: page 55 (top); Image 3a02558: page 55 (bottom);
 Image 3a12743: page 58 (top left).
North Wind Archives: page 9; page 11; page 25 (bottom);
 page 41 (bottom).
Rex Features: page 49. Shutterstock: page 5 (top); page 8 (left);
 page 8 (top right); page 8 (bottom); page 18; page 20 (top right);
 page 27; page 27 (inset); page 43 (background); pages 50-51;
 pages 52-53 (bottom); page 57.
Superstock: page 20 (bottom right).
Wikipedia (public domain): page 5 (bottom); page 17 (top); page
 33; page 54; page 56 (bottom).

Library and Archives Canada Cataloguing in Publication

Thomas, William, 1947-
 William Lloyd Garrison : a radical voice against
slavery / William David Thomas.

Voices for freedom: abolitionist heros)
Includes index.
ISBN 978-0-7787-4825-0 (bound).--ISBN 978-0-7787-4841-0 (pbk.)

 1. Garrison, William Lloyd, 1805-1879--Juvenile literature.
2. Abolitionists--United States--Biography--Juvenile literature.
3. Antislavery movements--United States--History--19th century--
Juvenile literature. I. Title. II. Series: Voices for freedom:
abolitionist heros

E449.G25T46 2009   j973.7'114092   C2009-904189-8

Library of Congress Cataloging-in-Publication Data

Thomas, William, 1947-
 William Lloyd Garrison : a radical voice against slavery /
William David Thomas.
 p. cm. -- (Voices for freedom: abolitionist heros)
Includes index.
 ISBN 978-0-7787-4841-0 (pbk. : alk. paper) -- ISBN 978-0-7787-
4825-0 (reinforced library binding)
1. Garrison, William Lloyd, 1805-1879--Juvenile literature.
2. Abolitionists--United States--Biography--Juvenile literature.
3. Antislavery movements--United States--History--19th century--
Juvenile literature. I. Title. II. Series.
 E449.G25T47 2010
 326'.8092--dc22
 [B]
                                                  2009027270

Crabtree Publishing Company
www.crabtreebooks.com   1-800-387-7650
Copyright © **2010 CRABTREE PUBLISHING COMPANY.** All rights reserved. No part of this publication may be reproduced, stored in
a retrieval system or be transmitted in any form or by any means, electronic, mechanical, photocopying, recording, or otherwise, without
the prior written permission of Crabtree Publishing Company.

**Published
in Canada
Crabtree Publishing**
616 Welland Ave.
St. Catharines, Ontario
L2M 5V6

**Published in
the United States
Crabtree Publishing**
PMB16A
350 Fifth Ave., Suite 3308
New York, NY 10118

**Published in the
United Kingdom
Crabtree Publishing**
Maritime House
Basin Road North, Hove
BN41 1WR

**Published
in Australia
Crabtree Publishing**
386 Mt. Alexander Rd.
Ascot Vale (Melbourne)
VIC 3032

Contents

It had been five years since William Lloyd Garrison had seen his mother. He had changed a great deal since they had parted. He had grown to full adult height. Although his hair was thick and dark, it was already beginning to recede from his forehead. That, and the glasses he had recently started to wear, made Garrison look older than his 18 years. Garrison lived in Newburyport, Massachusetts, where he was learning the printing business. His mother worked as a nurse for wealthy families in Baltimore, Maryland. As he traveled to meet her, he wondered if his mother would recognize him. He would soon discover that Francis Garrison had changed even more than he had.

Henny

When he arrived in Baltimore in 1824, Garrison was shocked at his mother's appearance. "I found her in tears..." he wrote, "so altered, so emaciated that I should never have recognized her." She had been a tall, strong woman, but now she was weak and frail. Her lungs were failing.

Garrison's mother, who had worked caring for others, needed someone to care for her. A family she knew sent a woman named Henny to stay with her. Henny did so. She had no choice. She was an African-American slave.

Above: The USS *Constellation*, the last all-sail ship built for the U.S. Navy, is shown here in Baltimore Harbor. The city was an important seaport in Garrison's time, and it still is today. The U.S. national anthem, "The Star Spangled Banner," was written about the siege of Fort McHenry, which is in Baltimore Harbor.

Right: This statue of William Lloyd Garrison is in a small park on Commonwealth Avenue, in Boston. The inscription on the side, including the words "I will be heard," is from the first issue of Garrison's newspaper, *The Liberator*.

Garrison had little experience with African Americans and even less with slaves. Newburyport, where he had lived most of his young life, had only a few black residents. All of them were free because slavery was illegal in Massachusetts. Although it was an issue Garrison knew little about then, it would soon become the driving force in his life. He would spend nearly 40 years speaking, writing, and nearly dying in his efforts to abolish slavery.

Slavery in America

There were slaves in America almost from the start of its colonization by Europeans. The first permanent settlement in the colonies was at Jamestown, Virginia. English settlers arrived there in 1607. By 1650, there were nearly 300 African slaves in Virginia. By 1675, ships were sailing regularly from America to Africa to buy, trade for, or kidnap men,

This 1835 illustration (left) shows captured Africans being chained and sent into the hold of a slave ship.

Shown below: actual shackles taken from a slave ship.

On Board a Slave Ship

The ships that carried slaves from Africa to America were not large. Since slave traders made a profit from each slave sold, the ships were always tightly packed with human cargo. Often 300 to 400 people—men, women, and children—were chained close together in cramped spaces. There was not enough room to stand. Often, there was not even enough room to sit up. There were no toilets. Although sometimes they were allowed to huddle on deck or forced to dance or exercise by the crew, most of the slaves' time was spent in the crowded hold, covered with their own waste and vomit. It was said that, at sea, a slave ship could be smelled before it was seen.

Africans kidnapped into slavery endured horribly cramped conditions on their voyages to America. This engraving shows men crowded onto the deck of a ship. Behind them, on an upper deck, are female slaves.

women, and children for slaves. Those who survived the voyage to the colonies were sold at public auctions, like cattle or furniture.

By the early 1700s, more and more slaves were arriving in the American colonies. The greatest numbers were used as farm laborers. Of these farm slaves, nearly all were the property of landowners in the southern colonies.

North and South

Almost from the beginning of European colonization, the North and the South differed on slavery. Farms in the North were small, and the work was seasonal. Crops like apples, corn, and potatoes needed a lot of work in spring

In the days before farm machinery, growing tobacco (left), cotton (above), and sugar cane (below) required a tremendous amount of hard labor. Most of that labor was provided by slaves.

and fall. There was less work in summer, and almost none during the snowy northern winters.

It was different in the South. The most common crops grown there—rice, sugar cane, and tobacco—required work year-round. By 1759, 90 percent of the slaves in America lived in the southern colonies. As agriculture expanded in the South—especially cotton growing—more slaves were needed.

As the number of slaves grew in the South, opposition to slavery began to grow in the North. Many religious groups opposed slavery, saying that it was against God's will for one person to own another. Also, many of the first states were inspired by the ideals of freedom and liberty that had been put forward as founding principles of the new United States of America. They marked their transition from colonies to states by ending slavery

Cotton and Slavery

The cotton grown in America was full of seeds and husks. These had to be removed before the cotton could be made into cloth. Cleaning the cotton by hand took so long that the crop was barely worth growing. In 1793, U.S. inventor Eli Whitney built a machine that could quickly clean cotton. It was called the cotton "gin"— short for engine. It allowed cotton to be grown profitably all across the South. The cotton gin increased the demand for cotton plantations, and that increased the demand for slaves.

In this old illustration, two slaves clean the seeds and husks from cotton using Whitney's "gin."

within their borders. By 1780, both Vermont and Massachusetts had made slavery illegal. Pennsylvania, New York, and New Jersey passed laws that would gradually free slaves living there.

Not everyone in the North opposed slavery. Many northerners did business with the southern states. Cotton, timber, and other raw materials from the South were needed in northern mills and factories. Slave labor allowed northerners to make higher profits.

Three-Fifths of a Person

In 1787, the U.S. Constitution—the document that would be the law of the land— was finalized, and in 1789 it went into effect. Article One described how the states would be represented in Congress. It gave each state a different number of representatives based on the state's population.

Men, women, and children—all slaves—are shown picking cotton in this illustration of a Georgia plantation.

Northerners argued that slaves should not be counted as part of a state's population. Southerners said they should. The two sides finally reached an agreement called the Three-Fifths Compromise. It counted each slave as three-fifths of a person. (Five slaves would equal three people.) The Compromise also said that the slave trade would end after 20 years. That meant owners could keep their current slaves, but no more would be allowed to enter the country. (The slave trade did in fact end in 1808, but it took a separate piece of legislation by Congress to bring this about.)

A Rush

The 20-year limit started a rush to acquire slaves while it was still legal. In a 10-year period, from 1798 to 1808, almost 200,000 more slaves were brought to the U.S. from Africa. Nearly all of them went to southern states. By 1810, there were more than one million slaves in the United States. In some of these states, slaves made up half of the population. In South Carolina, two-thirds of the state's people were slaves. The economy and way of life in the South were becoming dependent on slave labor.

Remember Her

William Lloyd Garrison had paid little attention to the growing debate about slavery. But now, visiting his mother in Baltimore, he was face to face with it. His mother was dying, and the only person caring for her was Henny, a slave.

Fanny Garrison described the kind and gentle care Henny gave her. She told Garrison,

> *Although a slave to man, [she is] yet a free-born soul by the grace of God... remember her for your poor mother's sake.*

His mother died soon after his visit. Garrison remembered her words and would soon take up the cause of Henny and every other "free-born soul" in the United States.

The Fugitive Slave Act

As the number of slaves in America grew, so did the number who tried to escape. In 1793, Congress passed the Fugitive Slave Act. It allowed slave hunters to capture escaped slaves in any state or territory. To take the person away, all the hunter had to do was tell a judge the person was an escaped slave. The captured person was not allowed a trial. Most northern states opposed the Act and did little to enforce it. Some states passed laws protecting freed blacks. This increased the ill feelings between northern and southern states.

The heartbreak caused by slave hunters is shown in this hand-colored woodcut. African-American families were often torn apart by these men.

CHAPTER TWO

Apprentice

William Lloyd Garrison's story starts with Abijah Garrison, an immigrant merchant sailor from New Brunswick, Canada. One Sunday, Abijah's ship was anchored near a small town in Maine. He went to the local church.

Miss Blue Jacket

There he saw a tall, dark-haired girl wearing a blue dress and jacket. Garrison followed her home, calling her "Miss Blue Jacket." Her name was Francis Lloyd, but she was called Fanny by her friends and family. Garrison began writing to her and visited when he could. In December 1798, they were married.

The Garrisons moved to Canada. Their son James was born in 1801, followed by a daughter, Caroline, in 1803. The next year, the family moved to Newburyport, Massachusetts. There, in 1805, their second son was born. His full name was William Lloyd Garrison, but his mother always called him Lloyd.

Hard Times

The year 1808 was a hard one for the family. Abijah couldn't find work. Lloyd's sister Caroline died suddenly. Two months later, a new sister, Maria, was born. For a long time, Lloyd's father had been drinking heavily. One night Fanny angrily chased him from the house. They never saw him again.

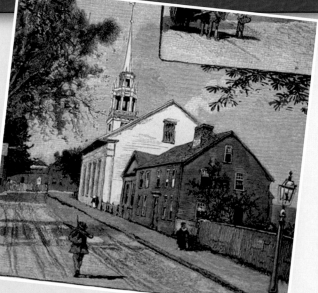
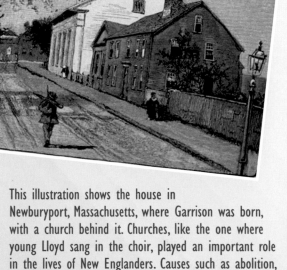

This illustration shows the house in Newburyport, Massachusetts, where Garrison was born, with a church behind it. Churches, like the one where young Lloyd sang in the choir, played an important role in the lives of New Englanders. Causes such as abolition, temperance, and education were promoted by churches.

Fanny Garrison was a strong woman, with great Christian faith. She went to work to support herself and her children. She became a nurse, caring for the children and sick adults in wealthier families. A friend, Mrs. Farnham, shared her home with the Garrisons.

Money was very scarce. To help meet family needs, Fanny made molasses candy and sent young Lloyd out on the streets to sell it. Sometimes he took a bucket and begged for food scraps at wealthy homes. Lloyd never forgot those hard times, but he also remembered singing hymns with his mother. They gave her strength, and she passed that strength on to him.

Separated

In 1811, Fanny moved to Lynn, a town about 25 miles (40 kilometers) away. James, who was now 11 years old, became an apprentice in a shoe factory. Fanny worked as a nurse. Lloyd stayed in Newburyport with a man named Mr. Bartlett, the deacon of the Baptist church.

Lloyd enjoyed his time with the Bartlett family. He carried firewood, cared for Deacon Bartlett's apple trees, and sold apples in the fall. Sometimes he was able to go to school. Although young, he had a strong voice. Lloyd sang the hymns his mother taught him in the church choir on Sundays.

The family was reunited in 1815, when Lloyd was ten. The shoe factory in Lynn, where James worked, moved to Baltimore, Maryland. The Garrison family moved with it. Fanny continued nursing while Lloyd joined James in the shoe factory. They worked from sunrise to sunset, and both boys hated it. At last, James could stand it no longer. At age 14, he signed on a ship and sailed away. It would be many years before anyone saw him again.

Lloyd begged to return to Newburyport. Mrs. Garrison, perhaps fearing she would lose him as well, let him go back to Deacon Bartlett's. There, Lloyd did chores, went to school when he could, and read every book he could find.

Learning a Trade

In December 1818, a sign went up in the window of the Newburyport newspaper, the *Newburyport Herald*. Ephraim Allen, the editor, wanted a boy to learn the printing trade. Just before he turned 14, Lloyd became a printer's apprentice.

He lived in Mr. Allen's house and worked at the newspaper six days a week. He swept floors, boiled varnish and lampblack to make ink, and cleaned the printing equipment. He watched the other workers setting type and using the printing presses. He remembered later, "It seemed to me that I should never be able to do anything of the kind." But he did.

Apprenticeships

Two hundred years ago, when Garrison was a boy, most goods were still made by hand. Furniture, window glass, shovels, ladies' dresses, and rifles were all made by skilled workers. There were no schools that taught those skills. Instead, trades were learned through apprenticeships. Young people, usually between 10 and 12 years old, were apprenticed to master craftsmen. They did whatever work their masters asked. In return, they were taught the trade and received food, clothing, and a place to sleep. Apprenticeships lasted from four to seven years. At the end of the time, the apprentice became a "journeyman." These trained workers would often travel from town to town, working short-term jobs, until they could earn enough to start their own business.

A young apprentice, learning shoemaking from a master craftsman, is shown in this painting by Emile Adan.

Lloyd learned to set type, starting with simple advertisements, then moving on to handbills and longer stories. Mr. Allen called him the best young printer he'd come across. That was high praise. After just two years, Allen made young Lloyd Garrison the foreman of his print shop.

This photograph from the 1920s shows a young typesetter at work. Note the number of different compartments in the type case.

An Old Bachelor

One day the *Herald* carried a story about a man who had been engaged to a woman for two years. When he refused to marry her, a judge fined the man $750. Garrison, who was too shy to even talk to girls, thought this was disgraceful. He disguised his handwriting and wrote a letter to the *Herald* about the case. Part of it said,

> *...women in this country are too ... puffed up and inflated with pride and self-conceit.... I am determined to live a single life and not trouble myself about the ladies.*

Garrison, who was 16, signed the letter "AOB—An Old Bachelor." He slipped it under the door of the newspaper office and waited.

Next day, Mr. Allen found the letter. He liked it and read it out loud to everyone. Then he handed it to Garrison and told him to set it in type. Garrison's first writing appeared in the *Herald* the next day.

Over the next two years, more letters from "AOB" appeared at the *Herald*. Mr. Allen printed them all. They were so popular that Allen finally printed a notice asking "AOB" to come to the office so he could meet him in person. Garrison then had to admit that the articles were his work.

Sticks and Galleys

In the 1820s, printing was a skilled and time-consuming business. Each letter and punctuation mark was an individual piece of metal. These pieces of "type" had to be assembled, one at a time, to make words, sentences, and paragraphs. The type was kept in a special case, with separate compartments for each letter and character.

All newspaper stories were written by hand, then given to the compositor. That was the person who "set" the type. He held a small metal tray, called a stick, in his left hand. As quickly as possible, he would reach into the type case, select the letters needed, and place them in the stick.

When the stick was full, the compositor placed it in a wooden tray called a galley. A full galley would be one page of the newspaper. The galley was tied tightly with string and placed in an iron frame called a chase. The type was then inked and a piece of paper pressed onto it. This "proof" page was checked. If errors were found, the galley would have to be taken apart and reset. If the proof was good, the galley went to the press. After printing, each galley had to be cleaned. Then it was taken apart, letter by letter, and distributed back into the case.

Above: This "stick" of set type is resting on a type case. Note that the letters on the type are reversed. To a new typesetter, the letters "p," "b," and "d" look very much alike.

Below: binding a finished stick of type with a string. Other sticks will be joined with it to form a galley.

17

Rather than being angry, Mr. Allen was pleased. He gave Garrison a whole month off. Lloyd traveled to Baltimore, where he found his dying mother being cared for by Henny, the slave woman.

Fame

Garrison returned to Mr. Allen to finish the final two years of his apprenticeship. He learned more about the business and did a lot more writing. He especially began writing about politics and slavery.

Lloyd Garrison wanted to be noticed. He wanted his name to be known beyond Newburyport. He believed he could honor his mother that way. Garrison wanted fame, and he had an idea about how to get it.

Jail

CHAPTER THREE

Garrison finished his seven-year apprenticeship just after he turned 20. Mr. Allen offered him good pay to stay at the *Herald*, but Garrison wanted to start his own newspaper! Ephraim Allen liked young Garrison and wanted him to succeed. He helped him get a press and an office. Soon, Garrison's newspaper, which he called the *Newburyport Free Press*, was ready to go.

The *Newburyport Free Press*

In 1826, the first issue of the *Newburyport Free Press* hit the streets. It was a small, weekly paper with news, advertisements, editorials, and even some humor. During a July heat wave, for example,

A portrait of William Lloyd Garrison at age 20, about the time he began the *Newburyport Free Press*.

Garrison wrote, "Fat people look as if they would melt, and lean ones as if they would dry up!" Most of the stories in the *Free Press*, however, were serious. Many were about politics.

A Stormy Beginning

Soon after the *Free Press* began, former president Thomas Jefferson died. Garrison wrote a story that criticized Jefferson because he had owned slaves. This angered many people. Ephraim Allen wrote a story in his paper praising Jefferson's accomplishments. Garrison then wrote an editorial criticizing his former boss, who had done so much to help him.

Thomas Jefferson

Thomas Jefferson (1743–1826) is regarded among the greatest Americans. He wrote the Declaration of Independence and served as U.S. ambassador to France. As President, he approved the Louisiana Purchase, doubling the size of the United States. He then sent the Lewis and Clark expedition to explore and map these new lands. On the subject of slavery, however, Jefferson's words and actions were contradictory. He wrote that "all men are created equal" and that slavery was "an abominable crime." Yet Jefferson owned slaves until the day he died. For this reason alone, Garrison found Jefferson lacking.

A portrait of Thomas Jefferson (top left); Monticello, his home in Virginia (top right), which is now a museum; and restored slave quarters at Monticello.

Newspapers

Newspapers in Garrison's time were quite different than they are today. Most were printed just once a week. They were much smaller, usually one to eight pages. There were no photographs and very few illustrations. Nearly every town had its own newspaper. Large cities like Boston had eight or more. Newspapers often supported particular causes or political parties. People bought the paper they agreed with most.

Newspapers in the early 1800s often reported news in a way that reflected their own political or moral bias. This is a photograph of the front page of an anti-slavery newspaper called the *Genius of Universal Emancipation*. Garrison met its publisher, Benjamin Lundy, and wrote for the paper for a short time.

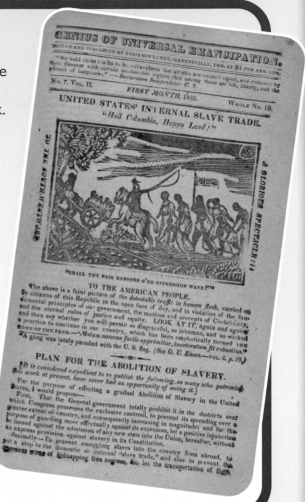

This was a sign of things to come. For most of his career, Garrison would attack, in print, anyone who did not completely agree with him. Something else he wrote in the *Newburyport Free Press* showed Garrison's future direction:

> *There is one theme which should be dwelt upon, till our whole country is free from the curse—it is SLAVERY.*

Blisters

Garrison decided that Newburyport was too small for someone with big ideas. To become well known and to use his name to further his causes, he needed to be in a bigger city. He headed for Boston. Garrison was so poor that he couldn't afford coach fare. He walked the 40 miles (64 km) to the city. It took him two days, and when he got there his feet were blistered and sore.

Garrison loved Boston. He could not find steady work, and he was often hungry, but he made a lot of new friends. He listened to famous speakers and preachers at the city's churches. Finally, in January 1828, he landed a job with a newspaper called the *National Philanthropist*.

The *Philanthropist* was a temperance newspaper. It reported news, but its real goal was to discourage people from drinking alcohol. Garrison wrote about temperance, but also about gambling and war. Most often, he wrote about slavery. The *Philanthropist*'s readers were not concerned with slavery. They believed it was a problem for the South, not them. After just six months, Garrison was fired.

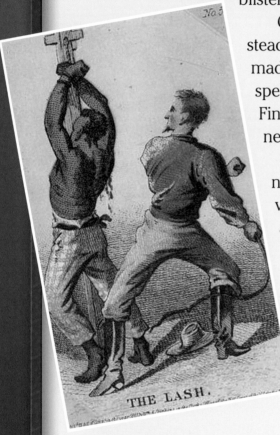

THE LASH.

This painting by American artist Henry Louis Stephens, called "The Lash," was one of a series of anti-slavery trading cards from the 1800s about the life of a slave. It clearly shows the brutal treatment some slaves received from their owners. Pictures like this were used by abolitionists to convince people that slavery should be stopped.

Opened Eyes

By now, Garrison's religious beliefs were controlling his life. He believed that America was a sinful place and that God wanted him to change it. In Boston, he met someone who felt the same way.

In March 1828, Garrison listened to a speech given by an abolitionist named

The Temperance Movement

The temperance movement was an attempt to stop, or try to control, alcohol consumption. The movement reached the United States in the early 1800s and was supported by many churches. Women—wives and mothers who had been hurt by men's uncontrolled drinking—were the most active temperance workers. Businesses later joined them. They too were being hurt by men's drinking.

In the 1800s, a strong connection existed between many of the reform movements of the day, including temperance, abolitionism, and women's suffrage (the right of women to vote). Many of the targets of these movements were perceived as social evils that undercut the ideals of the American Revolution and diminished the humanity of everyone living in the United States. In addition to sharing common goals with other reformers, many abolitionists, including Garrison, learned the techniques of reform while working for the temperance movement. Both movements relied on public speakers, newspapers, and the moral persuasiveness of religion to inspire people to embrace their causes.

Women played a major role in the temperance movement. The fanciful image above shows a woman as a knight, smashing barrels of liquor. Below, women sing hymns outside a saloon. Both pictures are from *Frank Leslie's Illustrated Newspaper*. It was published from 1855 until 1922.

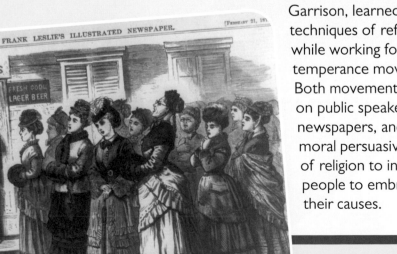

Benjamin Lundy. He was a Quaker who first witnessed slavery when he was 19. He saw men, women, and children being bought, sold, and marched away in chains. "My heart was deeply grieved," he later said, "and iron entered my soul."

Garrison said that Lundy "opened my eyes" and "inflamed my mind." He decided to dedicate his life to ending slavery. Lundy ran a newspaper in Baltimore called the *Genius of Universal Emancipation*. He needed help with it. Garrison went to Baltimore.

God-Given Color

Lundy and Garrison agreed that slavery was evil and had to be stopped. They disagreed, however, about how to do it. Lundy wanted to inform people about slavery. He was convinced that when people realized how terrible it was, they would end it. Garrison's approach was much more simple and direct: Free all slaves, and do it immediately.

Benjamin Lundy was afraid his readers would not accept such a radical idea, but Garrison would not back down. In one of his first articles, Garrison asked readers why Africans were kept as slaves. "Why," he wrote, "but because they are black?" He went on:

... is it a suitable cause for making men slaves, because God has given them such a color ... as He saw fit?

Benjamin Lundy, shown in this painting, visited 19 of the 24 states then in the United States. He traveled more than 12,000 miles (19,000 km)—many of them on foot—describing the evils of slavery.

The Slavery Debate

All across the northern states, groups had very different ideas about abolition. The most conservative of them believed that slavery should be decided on a state-by-state basis. Naturally, the pro-slavery southern states supported this idea.

   Moderate groups wanted to end slavery but argued about the best way to do it. Many northerners favored gradual emancipation, freeing slaves over many years. Some states had already passed laws requiring this. Other moderates said slave owners should be paid to free their slaves, but no one could agree on who should pay them. A few groups favored placing freed slaves in their own communities or even returning them to Africa.

Two images of slavery. Above: A mother and her daughter are forever separated when one is sold to a new owner. Below: Many pro-slavery groups used pictures like this to show that slaves were happy and well cared for.

   Behind many of these arguments was racism. Many northerners, even those who wanted to end slavery, did not want freed blacks living near them. They feared that ending slavery would send large numbers of unskilled, uneducated blacks northward. They believed freed slaves would take their jobs and change their communities.

   Radical abolitionists, like Garrison, wanted complete emancipation immediately. Many also favored giving blacks—and women—equal rights.

Lundy's readers were not used to being challenged like that. Soon, however, Garrison would give the readers an even greater challenge.

Found Guilty

In 1829, Garrison learned that a ship had just sailed from Baltimore carrying 75 slaves to plantations in the South. He also learned that the ship's owner, Francis Todd, was from his own hometown of Newburyport. Todd lived in one of the houses where Garrison had once begged for food.

Slavery was perfectly legal in Baltimore, and selling slaves south was also legal. Despite these facts, Garrison took a strongly moral position against Todd's actions. Quickly writing an angry story for the *Genius*, Garrison said that Todd and the ship's captain were "highway robbers and murderers" who should be put in prison for life. Todd got a lawyer and sued Garrison for libel. At his trial, Garrison was found guilty and sentenced to six months in jail.

Garrison wrote many letters and stories while in jail. Newspapers all over the North printed them, and he became famous. One newspaper said that Garrison's only crime was to show how terrible slavery really was. When Garrison was finally released, he learned that people had stopped buying the *Genius* because of his radical writing and actions. He was without a job once more.

This woodcut of a chained slave was the seal of the Society for the Abolition of Slavery in England in the 1780s. The picture was also used in many publications in the United States.

Back to Africa

The American Colonization Society (ACS) was founded in 1816. The ACS wanted to start colonies of former slaves in Africa and on Caribbean islands. Garrison joined the Society in 1830. He soon realized that the group was not concerned with the welfare of former slaves. Some of its members were actually slave owners! They viewed freed black people as bad influences on slaves and simply wanted them removed from the United States. Others—mostly northerners—felt that freed black people would compete with poor white people for jobs. Still others, while more sympathetic to African Americans, were nonetheless racist in their own right. They felt that freed black people would not be able to compete in a free society.

Garrison quit the Society and later wrote many articles criticizing it. The ACS had one success, however. It started a colony in Africa which, in 1847, became the nation of Liberia.

When areas settled by freed black people from the United States became the African nation of Liberia (shown circled on map), the citizens of that newly independent country chose a design for their flag (inset) that bore similarities to that of the United States. Liberia today has a population of more than 3,300,000. Through most of its history, Liberia has been a troubled nation characterized by corruption and warfare.

CHAPTER FOUR

The Liberator

Garrison left Baltimore and traveled around the North, giving speeches and meeting people. Many of them were freed black people. In this respect, Garrison was different from many other abolitionists. Few of them actually associated with black people. Garrison did. He spoke in their churches and attended their meetings. In return, many black families gave Garrison food and a place to sleep while he traveled. At last, Garrison returned to Boston. He wanted to start another newspaper, one dedicated to ending slavery.

A portrait of Garrison as he looked during the years he published *The Liberator*.

THE LIBERATOR.

VOL. I.] WILLIAM LLOYD GARRISON AND ISAAC KNAPP

BOSTON, MASSACHUSETTS.] OUR COUNTRY IS THE WORLD—OUR COUNTRYMEN ARE M

Above: The "masthead" from an early issue of *The Liberator*. Note that both Garrison and Isaac Knapp are named as publishers. Knapp was a friend who had worked with Garrison on the *Newburyport Free Press*. They eventually quarreled over Knapp's bookkeeping and Garrison fired him.

Right: A portrait of the Reverend Samuel May, a prominent abolitionist who helped start a number of anti-slavery societies. He also helped Garrison get *The Liberator* started.

Far right: The front page of the April 23, 1831, edition of *The Liberator*, published several months after the paper's founding in January 1831.

Samuel J. May.

A New Beginning

Garrison's first task was to raise money. He needed subscribers signed up to buy his newspaper before he could begin to print it. Garrison gave speeches and wrote letters to people across the North to attract supporters. The Reverend Samuel May, a well-known abolitionist, helped him.

Orders for the newspaper finally began to arrive. Among them was an order from James Forten, an African-American sail maker in Philadelphia. Forten ordered not one but 27 subscriptions! At last, Garrison had enough money to begin. He got a press, rented a small office, sat down, and began to write.

I Will Be Heard

Garrison called his paper *The Liberator*. It was a bold title, and it reflected his goal to liberate, or free, all slaves. Reverend May suggested other names that sounded less militant, but Garrison would not listen. Once his mind was made up, almost nothing could change it.

The first issue of *The Liberator* appeared on January 1, 1831. It was small, just four pages, and was printed on cheap paper with poor ink. Its message, however, was crystal clear. The subject was ending slavery. Garrison wrote the words shown to the right:

> "I will be as harsh as the truth, as uncompromising as justice. On this subject I do not wish to think, or speak, or write with moderation ... urge me not to use moderation in a cause like the present. I am in earnest....
> I will not excuse—I will not retreat a single inch—
> AND I WILL BE HEARD."

Fame and Threats

Garrison gave away copies of his newspaper to get more readers. He even mailed copies to the editors of newspapers in the South. They, in turn, wrote blistering articles, attacking Garrison and his views. That was fine with Garrison—it was free publicity! "My language... will displease many," he wrote. "To displease them is my intent."

In the summer of 1831, eight months after he started publishing, there was a deadly uprising of slaves in Virginia. Many southerners

Nat Turner's Rebellion

Nat Turner was a Virginia slave, known as a preacher. Other slaves called him "the Prophet." In August 1831, Turner had a vision telling him to lead an armed rebellion. With four other slaves, he stole weapons and killed his owner and the owner's entire family. More slaves joined Turner, and in two days they killed nearly 60 white people. Soldiers captured the gang, but Turner escaped for several weeks. At last he was caught, tried, and hanged.

Turner's rebellion spread great fear among southern white people. They retaliated by killing nearly 200 black people, most of them innocent slaves. In addition, even greater restrictions were placed on African Americans, both slaves and freed black people.

This drawing of Nat Turner's rebellion, showing white women and children about to be slaughtered, was designed to enrage and frighten white people in the South.

blamed Garrison for it, saying his ideas had encouraged the revolt. Although Garrison was opposed to violence, he praised the courage of the slaves in *The Liberator*. He wrote these words (right):

> *I do not justify the slaves in their rebellion, yet I do not condemn them.... Of all men living, our slaves have the best reason to assert their rights by violent measures....*

Proponents, or supporters, of slavery struck back. A group in South Carolina offered a reward of $1,500 for the capture of anyone with a copy of *The Liberator*. North Carolina officials promised to arrest Garrison if he entered the state. The Georgia House of Representatives offered $5,000 to anyone who could capture Garrison and bring him to the South.

Doing God's Work

It was not just *The Liberator* that made Garrison known and hated. In 1833, he joined two New York City businessmen, brothers Arthur and Lewis Tappan, to start the American Anti-Slavery Society (AAS).

Branches of the organization soon appeared throughout the North. Members held meetings, gave lectures, sent letters to elected officials, and distributed booklets. Slave owners in the South and racists in the North regarded the Society's activities as a threat. Their speakers and meetings were often attacked by pro-slavery groups.

Garrison wasn't safe, even in Boston. He received hundreds of death threats in the mail. People tossed rocks and rotten eggs at his office. One morning he found a gallows had been built there. It did not deter him. Garrison truly believed that he was doing God's work, and that God would protect him. Nothing, however, could protect him from love.

Helen C. Garrison.

A portrait of Helen Benson.
Even before she married Garrison, Benson was very active in the Boston anti-slavery movement.

An Old Bachelor No More

Helen Benson was the sister of one of Garrison's abolitionist friends. She had blue eyes, light brown hair, and a gentle manner. William Lloyd Garrison, called by some the most hated man in America, fell in love.

Elijah Lovejoy (1802–1837)

Elijah Lovejoy was a deeply religious man who opposed slavery. In 1827, he moved to St. Louis, Missouri. There, he started a newspaper called the *St. Louis Observer*. He wrote articles condemning slavery. Lovejoy favored gradual emancipation. Missouri was a slave state, and Lovejoy's writing upset a lot of people. He received so many threats that he moved across the Mississippi River to Illinois, a free state. Slavery supporters followed him. In 1837, a mob attacked his office, destroyed his printing press, and murdered Lovejoy. His death upset people in the northern states and spurred many of them to join the abolitionist movement.

The attack on Elijah Lovejoy's newspaper is shown in this wood engraving. Lovejoy's murder increased support for abolition in the North.

The fiery, angry newspaperman wrote to Helen, "Your humility charms me, and your good sense and wise judgment.... Of course I love you." They were married in 1834. The Reverend Samuel May, who had helped Garrison launch *The Liberator*, performed the ceremony.

Riot

Six months later, in the summer of 1835, Garrison nearly died. A British abolitionist named George Thompson was touring the United States, calling for an immediate end to slavery. By the time he reached Boston, he had made a lot of enemies.

Thompson and Garrison were to speak together at a meeting of the Boston Female Anti-Slavery Society. A note warned Garrison that Thompson would be attacked. Garrison urged Thompson to leave. He did, but Garrison stayed.

A large crowd of angry men gathered outside the hall. The mayor of Boston and several police officers broke through the crowd and escorted the women out. The crowd then rushed in and found Garrison. They dragged him into the street with rope around his waist crying, "Lynch him!"

Garrison didn't struggle or show any fear. He stayed calm until the mayor and police returned. They offered Garrison protection, but only if he signed a paper saying he was responsible for causing a riot. Garrison signed and was put in a jail cell. That night he carved a message into the cell's wall. It said:

> *Wm. Lloyd Garrison was put into this cell ... to save him from the violence of a mob ... who sought to destroy him for preaching the ... doctrine that "all men are created equal.*

Above: George Thompson, the British abolitionist, became Garrison's close friend. Garrison's first son was named after him.

Left: Garrison was nearly killed by a mob in 1835. By most accounts, he was dragged off with a rope around his waist. In this painting, artist Morton Roberts showed the rope placed around Garrison's neck.

Separation

Not long after the riot, in February 1836, the Garrisons' first child was born. They named him George Thompson Garrison. The proud father wrote in his journal, "A fine little son was born to me this day ... for which precious gift I wish to thank God." The Garrisons eventually had seven children.

Garrison cheerfully took on the "burdens which most husbands and fathers shun," including diapers. He once said he "was born into the world to take care of babies." In the coming years he could often be found rolling on the floor of his home, playing with his children.

Garrison is shown in this photograph with his daughter Francis, called Fanny. She was named after Garrison's mother.

CHAPTER FIVE

Politics and Women

The American Anti-Slavery Society held its annual meeting in 1839. It soon became clear that differences were driving the group apart. The Tappan brothers, who had helped Garrison begin the AAS, believed that political action was the best way to end slavery. The Tappans and their supporters wanted to help elect anti-slavery candidates and pass new laws. Votes, they believed, would do more to end slavery than fiery writing or angry speeches.

Garrison refused to consider slavery a political issue. In his mind, it was a moral issue. It was a question of right and wrong, not laws. Garrison would not join any political party. Articles in *The Liberator* urged readers not to vote at all. He wrote that the government was immoral because it allowed slavery to exist, and voting supported that immoral government.

The two sides were also divided on women's issues. The more conservative AAS members felt it was improper for women to work alongside men or speak to mixed audiences. Many cited a Bible passage (I Corinthians 14:34) that says, "Let your women keep silence." Garrison had written articles in *The Liberator* in favor of women's rights. He hired women to work as typesetters at the paper. He and his followers insisted that women could join the Society, speak at meetings, and serve as officers in the organization.

Before the meeting ended, the Tappans and other conservatives had formed a new abolition society. Garrison and his followers continued with the AAS.

The image of the chained slave asking, "Am I not a man, and a brother?" was printed on the side of this box used to collect coins for the Massachusetts Anti-Slavery Society.

Harriet Beecher Stowe and *Uncle Tom's Cabin*

Harriet Beecher Stowe (shown at right) was a schoolteacher, not given to public speaking or calling attention to herself. Yet this quiet woman made a great contribution to the cause of abolition. With the publication of her novel *Uncle Tom's Cabin* in 1852, she became a source of inspiration to other abolitionists, including two of the movement's most important leaders, William Lloyd Garrison and Frederick Douglass. *Uncle Tom's Cabin* told the story of a group of slaves, one of whom gives his life to save the others. The book quickly became hugely popular, selling more than 300,000 copies that year. The sentimental story helped people understand the human issues involved in slavery and brought many of them over to the abolitionist cause.

This illustration from Harriet Beecher Stowe's *Uncle Tom's Cabin* shows Tom with Little Eva. Even though Eva's father owns Tom, the two form a tender, loving friendship. The power of Tom's story made Stowe's novel an important component in the fight against slavery.

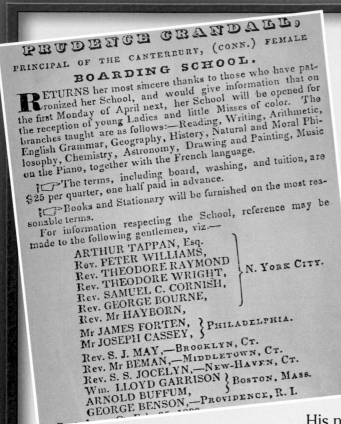

PRUDENCE CRANDALL,
PRINCIPAL OF THE CANTERBURY, (CONN.) FEMALE
BOARDING SCHOOL.

RETURNS her most sincere thanks to those who have patronized her School, and would give information that on the first Monday of April next, her School will be opened for the reception of young Ladies and little Misses of color. The branches taught are as follows:—Reading, Writing, Arithmetic, English Grammar, Geography, History, Natural and Moral Philosophy, Chemistry, Astronomy, Drawing and Painting, Music on the Piano, together with the French language.

☞ The terms, including board, washing, and tuition, are $25 per quarter, one half paid in advance.

☞ Books and Stationary will be furnished on the most reasonable terms.

For information respecting the School, reference may be made to the following gentlemen, viz.—

ARTHUR TAPPAN, Esq.
Rev. PETER WILLIAMS,
Rev. THEODORE RAYMOND
Rev. THEODORE WRIGHT,   } N. YORK CITY.
Rev. SAMUEL C. CORNISH,
Rev. GEORGE BOURNE,
Rev. Mr HAYBORN,
Mr JAMES FORTEN,   } PHILADELPHIA.
Mr JOSEPH CASSEY,
Rev. S. J. MAY,—BROOKLYN, CT.
Rev. Mr BEMAN,—MIDDLETOWN, CT.
Rev. S. S. JOCELYN,—NEW-HAVEN, CT.
Wm. LLOYD GARRISON } BOSTON, MASS.
ARNOLD BUFFUM,
GEORGE BENSON,—PROVIDENCE, R. I.

This notice appeared in *The Liberator* in 1833. Prudence Crandall was advertising her school for "young Ladies and little Misses of color." Note that she lists Arthur Tappan and Garrison as references.

Listening to a Piece of Property

In 1841, Garrison met an escaped slave who was living in New Bedford, Massachusetts. The man earned very little, but he spent some of his money to subscribe to *The Liberator*. His name was Frederick Douglass.

Garrison listened in horror as Douglass described his life as a slave. He arranged to have Douglass speak at an abolitionist meeting. Few in the white audience had ever heard a former slave speak. They listened in shocked silence to his stories of whippings, humiliation, and forced separation from his family. When Douglass was finished, Garrison leaped up and shouted out a question:

"Have we been listening to a thing, a piece of property, or to a man?"

The crowd shouted back, "A man!"

"Shall such a man ever be sent back to slavery?"

"No!" was the loud response.

Frederick Douglass became famous almost overnight. He joined the Anti-Slavery Society and spoke at abolitionist meetings across the North. Another powerful voice had joined Garrison's in the fight to end slavery.

Frederick Douglass (1817–1895)

Frederick Douglass (shown here) was born into slavery in Maryland. Although it was illegal to teach a slave to read or write, Douglass learned with help from his master's wife and children. He worked on plantations, then was sent to Baltimore to work in a shipyard. In 1838, Douglass escaped slavery by means of trains and ships that brought him to New York. The next year he married a free black woman and moved to Massachusetts. There he met William Lloyd Garrison.

For four years Douglass traveled and spoke to anti-slavery groups. In 1845, his life's story was published. *The Narrative Life of Frederick Douglass: an American Slave* made him even more famous. Afraid that he might be caught and returned to slavery, Douglass fled to England. English Quakers raised money to buy his freedom. He returned to the United States in 1847 and moved to Rochester, New York. There, he started his own abolitionist newspaper, the *North Star*.

In 1853, Douglass argued with Garrison. He felt that blacks, not whites, should be leading the abolition movement. Unlike Garrison, he favored using politics to end slavery. He worked to pass laws aimed at helping free blacks. After the Civil War, he was named to several political posts. Douglass continued to fight for equal rights all of his life.

The Compromise of 1850

For several years, arguments had raged in Congress about admitting new states to the Union. Should they be free states or slave states? In 1849, when California wanted statehood, the debate became intense. Southern states began to talk about seceding—leaving the Union. An agreement was finally reached. The Compromise of 1850 admitted California as a free state. As a balance, it also reinforced the Fugitive Slave Act. The law made it the responsibility of the federal government rather than state governments to return fugitive slaves. It also required citizens of free states to help capture and return escaped slaves.

In *The Liberator*, Garrison raged against the Compromise, calling it a "covenant with slavery." He also had an answer to the southern states' threats to secede. Garrison wanted to beat them to it.

No Union!

Garrison concluded that the U.S. government accepted slavery. The northern states, as part of the Union, were being forced to accept it as well.

In his later years, Frederick Douglass was appointed Marshal of Washington, D.C., by President Hayes. In this drawing from *Frank Leslie's Illustrated Newspaper*, April 7, 1877, Douglass is shown being congratulated by former slaves.

The Underground Railroad

The Underground Railroad was a secret network of people who helped slaves reach freedom. "Conductors" on the railroad led small groups of escaped slaves through forests and along rivers, usually at night. Secret codes in stories and songs helped them find their way. Harriet Tubman, herself an escaped slave, was the most famous of these conductors. She led more than 300 slaves to freedom.

Frederick Douglass directed Rochester's Underground Railroad, helping escaped slaves reach freedom in Canada. "Stations" on the railroad were safe places where escapees could rest along the way. Churches and homes—some with hidden rooms—were used. From 1820 to 1860, as many as 4,000 "passengers" may have traveled north on the Underground Railroad.

Harriet Tubman in a photo thought to have been taken in the 1860s, when Tubman would have been in her 40s.

In this hand-colored woodcut, a burning torch lights the dark night for a group of escaping slaves along the Underground Railroad.

His solution to this problem was dramatic. Garrison began calling for the North to leave the Union! "I am not for slavery and union!" he said.

The front page of *The Liberator* carried a large headline: "Dissolution Now."

THE LIBERATOR.

DISSOLUTION NOW

In every speech he made, Garrison kept hammering at the idea. "No union with slaveholders" became his new motto. People of the free states, he said, should "demand the repeal of the Union or the abolition of slavery, not as a threat, but as a moral obligation."

Even for Garrison's friends and fellow abolitionists, this was an extreme position. It was typical of him, however. Garrison was nearly always certain about what was right. In his view, anything that differed from that was wrong. Not just a little bit wrong, but totally and completely wrong. He was an unrelenting, single-minded man.

Emancipation

CHAPTER SIX

Early in 1854, an angry debate was underway in the United States. It was about the territories of Kansas and Nebraska. The South wanted them open to slavery. The North wanted them free. Garrison, as always, said that slavery was immoral. He went further and said that the debate itself was wrong.

A Damning Sin

In February of that year, Garrison spoke to a large crowd in New York City. He said that those who argued against extending slavery in the territories were missing the point. If it was wrong to allow slavery into new places, then it was wrong to have it in the first place. "If slavery is not wrong," he asked the New Yorkers, "why has your state abolished it?"

He went on,

> *If it would be a damning sin to permit another Slave State into the union, why is not a damning sin to permit a Slave State to remain in the union?*

At end of the speech Garrison received a standing ovation. The next day, the *New York Times* printed the text of his speech. This was a mark of progress. Four years earlier, Garrison had nearly been run out of New York for expressing the same ideas.

Despite the best efforts of Garrison and others, the Kansas-Nebraska Act passed in May 1854. The Act said both territories could decide for themselves to be free or slave. *The Liberator* raged against this. Garrison called the Act "diabolical." How, he asked, could the government support such laws when so many were against them? Very soon, Garrison would have even more reason to criticize the government.

Chains and Bayonets

Anthony Burns was an escaped slave, hiding in Boston. Just days after the Kansas-Nebraska Act was passed, Burns was arrested by U.S. marshals. He was chained and put in jail. Abolitionists surrounded the courthouse in protest. President Franklin Pierce sent in soldiers with cannons to restore order.

A week later, large crowds watched as this single black man was marched through the streets. Burns was taken to an armed U.S. Navy ship, wrapped in chains, and surrounded by hundreds of soldiers. One newspaper said that catching Burns and returning him to slavery cost the U.S. government $100,000. *The Liberator's* headline said, "Slave Hunting at the Point of a Bayonet." Garrison wrote that these actions "converted a man into a thing." The Declaration of Independence said

This illustration from 1854 shows a portrait of Anthony Burns surrounded by drawings of events in his life. At the top right he is marched through the streets of Boston in chains.

"all men are created equal." Garrison wrote that Burns' treatment made the Declaration "a lie."

Burning

At a Fourth of July rally in 1854, 3,000 people showed up to hear Garrison speak. He talked about the U.S. Constitution, which allowed slavery. "This is the source and parent of all other atrocities," he said. He called the Constitution "a covenant with death and an agreement with hell!" Garrison then held up a copy of the Constitution, took out a match, and set it on fire. "So perish all compromises with tyranny!" he shouted. The crowd replied, "Amen."

As Garrison made speeches, the country was moving closer to civil war. Pro-slavery and anti-slavery groups were battling each other in Kansas. A fierce abolitionist named John Brown fought there and then moved east. In 1859, he attacked a U.S. Army arsenal in Virginia. His attack failed, but it created even more tension between North and South. Garrison did not approve of violence, but he praised Brown's courage and devotion to the cause of abolition.

Frank Leslie's Illustrated Newspaper

This picture of abolitionist John Brown appeared on the front page of *Frank Leslie's Illustrated Newspaper* in November 1859, shortly before Brown was executed for treason following his raid on the federal arsenal at Harpers Ferry.

War

The abolitionists who favored politics had helped form a new party, the Republicans. In 1860, that party nominated Abraham Lincoln to run for president. Although Lincoln had never been an abolitionist, he had always hated slavery and opposed its expansion. After his election, the southern states prepared to leave the Union. On April 14, 1861, southern forces attacked Fort Sumter, a U.S. Army post in South Carolina. The Civil War had begun.

Garrison was a pacifist. He had always opposed violence and war. Now he felt he had to support the Union cause, even though he did not always support Abraham Lincoln, whose main priority was the preservation of the Union. Garrison thought Lincoln's first priority should be ending slavery. He called the president "wishy-washy" for moving too slowly on that issue. Lincoln, he said, "had better be at his old business of splitting rails than at the head of a government like ours...."

Freedom

Lincoln finally made the move that Garrison had prayed for. On January 1, 1863, the president issued the Emancipation Proclamation, which freed

His Soul Goes Marching On

John Brown was born in Connecticut in 1800. His father was a very religious man who strongly opposed slavery. John carried on those beliefs. For years, Brown moved about the country, working at many different jobs, but always speaking against slavery. In 1849, he moved to a small black community called North Elba. It was deep in the

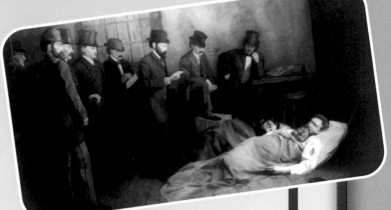

This painting shows an artist's version of a wounded John Brown, lying on the floor as his death sentence is read to him.

mountains of northern New York. There, Brown was active in the Underground Railroad, helping escaped slaves to freedom in Canada.

In 1855, he and five of his sons went to Kansas. They joined the fight against slavery in that territory. Brown led attacks against pro-slavery groups that killed several people. In 1859, Brown and a group of men attacked the U.S. Army arsenal at Harpers Ferry, Virginia. His plan was to steal weapons and use them to create an army of freed slaves. Soldiers quickly surrounded the gang. Fighting broke out, and all of Brown's men were killed or captured. Brown was tried for treason. He was hanged in December 1859. His body was returned to North Elba.

A song written about John Brown quickly became popular with anti-slavery groups across the North. Part of it went as follows:

"He captured Harpers Ferry with his 19 men so true. He startled Old Virginia till she trembled through and through. They hung him for a traitor, they themselves the traitor crew. But his soul goes marching on. Glory, Glory, Hallelujah, his soul goes marching on."

the slaves in the states that had seceded from the Union and formed the Confederate States of America. So this document freed most—but not all—slaves. Garrison joined with others in Boston, celebrating throughout the day. He set a headline in *The Liberator* in large type:

> *THE PROCLAMATION*
> *Three Million of Slaves Set Free!*
> *Glory Hallelujah!*

Despite his joy at Lincoln's actions, the war soon became serious and deeply personal for Garrison. His eldest son, George, wanted to join the Army. For a life-long believer in non-violence like Garrison, this was difficult. Father and son talked for hours. Garrison did not agree with his son's views, but he respected them.

George went off to war.

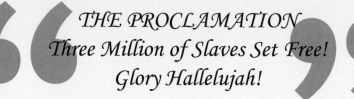

This bronze sculpture by artist Thomas Ball is in Washington, D.C. It shows Lincoln reading the Emancipation Proclamation to a slave whose chains are broken. The model for the slave was Archer Alexander, the last person caught under the Fugitive Slave Act. Some people have criticized the work because it shows an African American kneeling before Lincoln.

The 54th and Glory

The 54th Massachusetts Volunteer Infantry was formed in February 1863. Although its officers were white, all of the soldiers were black. It was one of the first black regiments ever formed.

The 54th Massachusetts was commanded by Colonel Robert Gould Shaw, a man from an abolitionist family in Boston. Two of Frederick Douglass's sons were in the regiment. The 54th was sent to South Carolina to take Fort Wagner, a Confederate stronghold. In the attack, more than 250 of them were killed, including Colonel Shaw. Private William Carney received the Congressional Medal of Honor for his bravery that day. It is the nation's highest military award. Carney was the first African American to be awarded it. In 1989, the story of the 54th was made into a popular film called *Glory*.

Following the creation of the 54th, a second all-black unit, the 55th Massachusetts, was formed to accommodate the large number of recruits. William Lloyd Garrison's eldest son, George, was one of the white officers who commanded this outfit.

Actor Morgan Freeman (center) starred in the film *Glory*. Actor Denzel Washington also had a major role.

CHAPTER SEVEN

Legacy

In 1864, the Republicans chose Abraham Lincoln to run for re-election as president. Garrison was invited to speak at their convention in Baltimore. That was where he'd been jailed for libel many years before. Garrison tried to visit his old cell, but the jail had been torn down. A new prison stood in its place.

Meeting Mr. Lincoln

When the convention ended, Garrison traveled to Washington, D.C., to congratulate Lincoln. When they met, Lincoln said he'd heard of Garrison's attempt to re-visit his old jail cell. "Then you couldn't get out," Lincoln joked, "now you cannot get in!"

Garrison and the president had a long talk. Though he had often criticized Lincoln in the past, Garrison now told him, "Since the Emancipation Proclamation, I have given you my hearty support and confidence."

The War Ends

By early 1865, northern troops had captured much of the South. This included Fort Sumter, in South Carolina, where the war had begun. A flag-raising ceremony was planned to mark the fort's return to Union control.

Garrison was invited to speak. As his ship arrived, word reached the passengers: The South had surrendered. The war was over! A band on the ship played "The Star Spangled Banner." When Garrison stepped off the ship, several thousand former slaves stood waiting on the shore to greet him.

The Emancipation Proclamation and the Thirteenth Amendment

Lincoln's Emancipation Proclamation freed most slaves, but it extended only to the states that were in rebellion against the government—the states that had joined the Confederacy. Delaware, Kentucky, Maryland, and Missouri—all slave states that had stayed within the Union during the Civil War—were not affected by the Emancipation Proclamation. Neither was West Virginia, which had broken free from Virginia and joined the Union in 1863 after deciding to gradually abolish slavery.

The Thirteenth Amendment to the U.S. Constitution, which was approved by Congress in 1865, freed all the slaves, forever. It said: "Neither slavery nor involuntary servitude ... shall exist within the United States." Each southern state was required to sign the new amendment before it could rejoin the Union. Garrison wrote a headline for *The Liberator* that read, "Hallelujah! Praise be to God!"

Through Your Labors

The next day Garrison attended services in an African-American church. A former slave named Samuel Dickerson stood up with two young girls. They were his daughters, he explained, but they had been sold and taken away from him. Now they were

Abraham Lincoln (1809–1865)

Abraham Lincoln grew up in a one-room log cabin with a dirt floor. He went on to become a lawyer and the 16th president of the United States. He guided the nation though its most difficult time and is counted among the greatest of America's presidents. Just weeks after the Civil War ended in 1865, Lincoln was shot and killed by a southern supporter named John Wilkes Booth. Garrison printed *The Liberator* with a black border around its pages. He wrote, "... no man ever did so large a business ... in the service of freedom and humanity."

This statue in Senegal both recalls the time when millions of Africans were taken from their homelands in chains and celebrates Senegal's status as a free nation in West Africa.

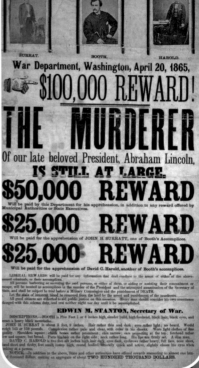

A reward poster for John Wilkes Booth and his accomplices. Twelve days after shooting Lincoln, Booth was killed trying to escape from soldiers in Virginia.

all free and reunited. Dickerson looked at Garrison and said, "Now sir, through your labors and those of your friends, they are mine. They are my daughters, and no man can take them from me." Garrison was then lifted on the shoulders of the congregation and paraded through the streets. He said it was the proudest moment of his life.

The Last *Liberator*

Garrison was 60 years old when the war ended. Abolition had succeeded. The slaves were free. His work was done. The final issue of *The Liberator* was printed in December 1865. Garrison was tired. He wrote, "Most happy am I to be no longer in conflict ... on the subject of slavery." Garrison also thanked his readers for their years of support.

The sad truth was that Garrison still needed their support. He had no money. He had never earned much and had put most of that back into the newspaper and other abolitionist causes. In gratitude for his work, his readers and friends started a retirement fund for Garrison. Many people made contributions, both large and small. One former slave sent a dollar to the fund, along with a note. It said,

> *If I were a millionaire ... I would give him $1,000,000 and make him President of the United States."*

William Lloyd Garrison in his later years.

Abolition and Women's Rights

In many ways, abolition was the seed from which the women's rights movement grew. Empowered by their work for the rights of slaves, many women continued to fight for their own rights.

Abby Kelley became an abolitionist after hearing Garrison speak. She joined the Anti-Slavery Society and spoke regularly at meetings. Her election to office helped cause the split in the AAS.

Angelina Grimké was a southern woman whose parents owned slaves, yet she took up the cause of emancipation. She was a brilliant writer and speaker. Garrison often printed her work in *The Liberator*.

In 1840, abolitionists Lucretia Mott and Elizabeth Cady Stanton went to London, England. They were the U.S. representatives to the World Anti-Slavery Conference. Initially not allowed to enter because they were women, they were eventually seated in a section with other women, roped off from the male participants. (Outraged by this decision by the male delegates, William Lloyd Garrison refused his seat with the male delegates and sat with the women.) Mott and Stanton began a campaign for women's rights. Together they planned a women's rights convention. It was finally held in 1848, in Seneca Falls, New York. This convention began the movement for women's suffrage in the United States.

Sojourner Truth, a former slave, spoke for both abolition and women's rights. Told once that women simply could not do what men could, Truth was reported to have replied: "Look at me! I could work as much and eat as much as a man ... and bear the lash as well. And ain't I a woman?"

In the 1800s, suffragists Elizabeth Cady Stanton (seated) and Susan B. Anthony were pioneers of the women's movement.

A Mournful Hour

In retirement, Garrison still spoke occasionally for women's rights or education for African-Americans. Helen, his wife for more than 40 years, died in 1876. Garrison left Boston then and moved to New York City to live with his daughter Fanny. His health grew worse and, surrounded by his children, he died on May 24, 1879.

Dozens of newspapers in the United States and Europe printed tributes. Frederick Douglass said, "This is a mournful hour." On the day he was buried, freed blacks across the nation gathered in churches and prayed for William Lloyd Garrison.

Wm. Lloyd Garrison 1874.

William Lloyd Garrison in 1874, at age 69.

Garrison was buried with his wife, Helen, beneath this simple tombstone in Forest Hills Cemetery, Jamaica Plain, Massachusetts. Eight friends, both white and black, carried his coffin. On the day of his funeral, flags were flown at half-staff all across Boston.

Making People Think

Garrison was a complicated man. Though deeply religious, he never belonged to a church. He was dedicated to non-violence, but he supported violent actions to end slavery. People who visited his office expected to find an angry, fire-breathing giant. Instead, they found a gentle, balding man who let a cat sleep on his shoulder as he wrote. Garrison was stubborn, rude, and often cruel to those who disagreed with him. He annoyed people, frightened people, and angered people. But most of all, he made people think about slavery. That, perhaps, was his greatest contribution.

Carry It On

Garrison's principles and ideas have been carried on by many people. Susan B. Anthony was one. She knew Garrison and worked for abolition. Later she led the struggle to get women the right to vote. Anthony once wrote, "Resistance to tyranny is obedience to God." Those words sounded much like Garrison's.

Mohandas Gandhi led India to independence through peaceful protest. Like Garrison, he was a deeply religious man, dedicated to non-violence, and he was relentless in the pursuit of his goals. Civil rights leader Martin Luther King, Jr., read Garrison's writings. He too was a religious man. King led a non-violent movement to win equal rights for African-Americans. Garrison urged people not to vote or support laws he believed were

This postage stamp from India commemorates Gandhi. He was murdered soon after India gained its independence in 1947.

immoral. This practice, first given the name "civil disobedience" in 1849 by American author Henry David Thoreau, was practiced by Anthony, Gandhi, and King, as well as by their numerous supporters. Like Garrison, all of them were threatened and arrested for the causes they believed in. And each of them, like Garrison, believed they would succeed in the end. A song from the days of King's civil rights movement expresses this:

> They can lock us up in prisons.
> All those prison walls will crumble.
> Every victory's gonna bring another.
> Carry it on, carry it on!

Anthony, Gandhi, and King carried on the spirit of *The Liberator*'s work. Others are doing it around the world today, for causes they believe in. That is the legacy of William Lloyd Garrison.

On August 28, 1963, Martin Luther King Jr. delivered his famous "I have a dream" speech to thousands of people gathered on The Mall in Washington, DC.

Chronology

1805 William Lloyd Garrison is born in Newburyport, Massachusetts.

1808 Garrison's sister Caroline dies; his sister Maria is born; his father Abijah abandons the family.

1811 Garrison's mother and brother move to Lynn, Massachusetts, so James can work in a shoe factory; Lloyd stays in Newburyport with Deacon Bartlett.

1815 The Garrison family moves to Baltimore; Lloyd and James work in a shoe factory.

1817 James runs away to sea; Garrison returns to Newburyport.

1818 Garrison begins his apprenticeship in the newspaper business at the *Newburyport Herald*.

1821 Garrison writes his first newspaper article, disguising himself as "An Old Bachelor."

1824 Garrison visits his dying mother in Baltimore.

1826 Garrison starts his own newspaper, the *Newburyport Free Press*; it fails in less than a year.

1827 Garrison leaves Newburyport for Boston.

1828 He is hired and fired as the editor of the *National Philanthropist* in Boston; he meets Benjamin Lundy.

1829 Garrison moves to Baltimore to work with Lundy on the *Genius of Universal Emancipation*.

1830 Found guilty of libel, Garrison is sentenced to six months in jail in Baltimore; returns to Boston; joins but later quits the American Colonization Society.

1831 On January 1, Garrison publishes the first issue of *The Liberator*; Nat Turner leads a slave rebellion in Virginia.

1833 The American Anti-Slavery Society is formed by Garrison and Arthur and Lewis Tappan.

1834 On September 4, Garrison marries Helen Benson.

1835 On October 21, rioters drag Garrison through the streets of Boston; he is held in jail for protection.

1836 George, the first of Garrison's seven children, is born.

1839 The American Anti-Slavery Society splits up due to disagreements about political action and participation by women.

1841 Garrison meets Frederick Douglass, a former slave.

1850 The Compromise of 1850 allows California to enter the Union as a free state but reinforces the Fugitive Slave Act.

1852 Harriet Beecher Stowe's anti-slavery novel, *Uncle Tom's Cabin*, is published.

1854 The Kansas-Nebraska Act passes; Garrison burns a copy of the U.S. Constitution at an anti-slavery rally.

1859 John Brown leads an attack on the arsenal at Harpers Ferry, Virginia.

1860 Abraham Lincoln is elected president; southern states secede from the Union and form the Confederate States of America.

1861 Southern forces attack and capture Fort Sumter, South Carolina, beginning the Civil War.

Chronology (cont.)

1863 President Lincoln issues the Emancipation Proclamation, freeing most slaves in the Confederacy.

1865 The Civil War ends; President Lincoln is assassinated; Garrison publishes the final issue of *The Liberator*.

1876 Helen Benson Garrison dies.

1879 William Lloyd Garrison dies at his daughter's home in New York at the age of 74.

Glossary

abolish To end, stop, or do away with something.

abolitionist A person who wanted to end slavery in America.

agriculture farming.

apprentice Someone who helps or works for a skilled worker while learning a trade.

arsenal A place where weapons and ammunition are made or stored.

atrocities Cruel or wicked actions.

colonization Sending groups of settlers to a place and establishing control over that place. Colonizing a region may also include establishing control over native people who live there.

compositor A person who sets type and lays out pages for a newspaper.

Confederate A person who fought for or supported the South during the Civil War.

congregation The members or people attending a church.

conservative Wanting things to stay the same or as they used to be.

covenant A formal agreement between people or groups.

deacon A church officer.

deter To stop or prevent.

diabolical Like or belonging to the devil; evil.

economy The wealth and resources of a nation or a region, especially as they provide jobs, money, goods, and services.

editor At a newspaper, the person who checks the accuracy of stories and decides what will be printed.

editorials Articles that express an opinion.

emaciated Extremely or dangerously underweight.

emancipation Freedom.

humiliation Being made to feel or look ashamed or unworthy.

humility Humbleness; a lack of arrogance or unearned pride.

legacy Something left behind, or handed down as a tradition.

legislation Laws, especially taken as a group.

libel Intentionally saying or writing something about a person that is untrue.

liberate To set free.

lynch To kill someone, especially by hanging, without a trial.

militant Very aggressive; acting in an angry manner.

moderate Not extreme; not too much or too little; calm.

moral Good or honest, having to do with what is right, not wrong.

ovation Applause or clapping.

pacifist A person who does not believe in and will not participate in violence or war.

proponents Those who support an idea or cause.

publicity Information given out to bring something to the attention of many people.

racism Thoughts, words or actions based on the belief that one race of people is better than another.

radical Favoring extreme or very unusual changes.

recede To move back or away from.

subscribers People who pay to receive a newspaper, magazine, or a service.

suffrage The right to vote.

temperance A movement to stop or strictly control drinking alcoholic beverages.

transition The process of changing over from one condition or state to another.

tributes Actions to show thanks or respect.

unrelenting Never weakening, stopping, or giving up.

varnish A liquid that puts a clear, hard coating on a surface.

Further Information

Books

Elliot, Henry. *Frederick Douglass: From Slavery to Statesman*
(Voices for Freedom: Abolitionist Heroes). Crabtree, 2010.

Hamilton, Virginia. *Many Thousands Gone: African Americans from Slavery to Freedom*. Knopf Books for Young Readers, 2002.

Horn, Geoffrey M. *John Brown: Putting Actions Above Words*
(Voices for Freedom: Abolitionist Heroes). Crabtree, 2010.

Hudson, Wade. *The Underground Railroad*. (Cornerstones of Freedom).
Children's Press, 2007.

Lantier, Patricia. *Harriet Tubman: Conductor on the Underground Railroad*
(Voices for Freedom: Abolitionist Heroes). Crabtree, 2010.

Stanchak, John. *Civil War* (DK Eyewitness Books). DK Publishing, Inc., 2000.

Web sites

www.sewanee.edu/faculty/Willis/Civil_War/documents/Liberator.html
This site shows the full text of the first issue of Garrison's newspaper,
The Liberator, including his famous statement "I will be heard!"

www.theliberatorfiles.com
Subscribe to *The Liberator*! This site has hundreds of articles from Garrison's
newspaper arranged by year and by subject. The site also includes biographical
information, some of Garrison's letters, a photo gallery, and more.

www.besthistorysites.net/USHistory_SouthSlavery.shtml
This site is designed for both teachers and students. It provides links to a wealth of
information on slavery in America. You can read the personal papers of Frederick
Douglass. Check out profiles of slaves living in both northern and southern
communities. Listen to the voices of former slaves in "American Slave Narratives."

www.nationalgeographic.com/railroad/j1.html
Take a ride on the Underground Railroad! Find out about the road to freedom
at this interactive Web site. It features history, people, timelines, possible routes,
a "Did You Know?" section, and a lot more.

http://tah.collaborative.org/NAEI/
The Northampton Association was established in 1842 as a community where men,
women, and children of all races could live, work, and learn. Garrison visited often.
Sojourner Truth lived there for a while. Learn about this great social experiment.

Index

About the Author

William David Thomas lives in Rochester, New York, a city that was a stop in the Underground Railroad and home of Frederick Douglass and Susan B. Anthony. Bill has written software documentation, training programs, annual reports, speeches, a song or two, lots of letters, and 30 books for children and young adults. He claims that he was once the King of Fiji but gave up the throne to pursue a career as a relief pitcher. It's not true.

Printed in the USA—BG